THE LAST INCANTATIONS

The Last Incantations

Poems

David Mura

TRIQUARTERLY BOOKS / NORTHWESTERN UNIVERSITY PRESS

EVANSTON, ILLINOIS

TriQuarterly Books
Northwestern University Press
www.nupress.northwestern.edu

Printed in the United States of America

10 9 8 7 6 5 4 3 2 1

Library of Congress Cataloging-in-Publication Data
Mura, David, author.
    The last incantations : poems / David Mura.
        pages cm.
    Includes bibliographical references.
    ISBN 978-0-8101-5237-3 (pbk. : alk. paper)
    I. Title.
  PS3563.U68L37 2014
  811'.54—dc23

                                                                    2013042252

♾ The paper used in this publication meets the minimum requirements of the American National Standard for Information Sciences—Permanence of Paper for Printed Library Materials, ANSI Z39.48–1992.

Contents

Acknowledgments

I wish to thank my friends who generously read and critiqued the entire manuscript: Ed Bok Lee, Juliana Pegues, and Bao Phi. I've received support and inspiration from my VONA colleagues Chris Abani, Elmaz Abinader, Junot Díaz, Ruth Foreman, Suheir Hammad, Mat Johnson, Diem Jones, and Willie Perdomo; from my Stonecoast MFA colleagues Annie Finch, Tim Seibles, Helen Peppe, and Patricia Smith; and from fellow writers Lauren K. Alleyne, Sun Mee Chomet, Martín Espada, Rachel Eliza Griffths, Lawrence Minh-Davis, Quincy Troupe, and Frank Wilderson. My brothers Alexs Pate and Garrett Hongo have been in my corner for years. Thanks to the late and beloved Lucille Clifton, mother to us all.

I wish to thank my editor, Parneshia Jones, for soliciting my manuscript and for her understanding and support of my work. Thank you to the staff at Northwestern University Press, particularly my copyeditor, Mike Ashby, and art director Marianne Jankowski.

I wish to thank my children, Tomo, Nikko, and Samantha, for their inspiration and love. My final thanks go to my wife, Susan Sencer, for tirelessly, patiently, and lovingly reading draft after draft of this manuscript. I could not have completed this without you, dear.

My thanks to the editors of the following publications, in which some of the poems previously appeared, sometimes in earlier versions.

The Asian American Literary Review: "Isamu Noguchi: Fragments from an Unwritten Memoir"

Black Renaissance Noire: "Poem for Patricia Smith upon My Nomination for the Urban Griots Award," "Dangerous Trains of Thought," "Song for an Asian American Radical: Yuri Kochiyama"

Cream City Review: "Summers with the JACL"

The Darfur Anthology: "General Roméo Dallaire, Commander of UNAMIR"

Drunken Boat: "Crystal" (sections I and II), "My Son at Ninth Grade," "Peter Wu's Poem"

Kartika Review: "Tales of Hybridity"

MARGIE/The American Journal of Poetry: "Last A.A. Incantation," "The Rape of Nanking"

Mizna: "Love Poem for Suheir Hammad"

Northwest Review: "Crystal" (section III)

Ploughshares: "The Left Panel of the Diptych Speaks"

PoetryMagazine.com: "Frightening Things"

The Seattle Review: "V.C.," "Wisconsin Hunting Season"

Spirituality & Health: "Aubade"

The Last Incantations

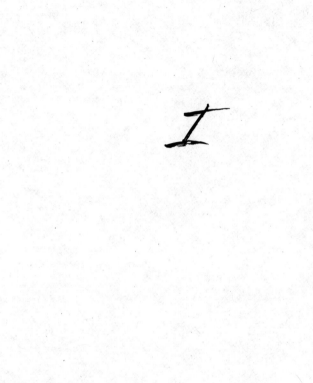

South Carolina Sea Island

A purple blush above the marshes; below
on the wooden deck, two boys squeal at the cage
of crabs they've yanked from the muddy inlet.
Each year we come back to this: a heron's white

cross sails towards the sea, the tide crawls out,
and a wasp sputters about the wooden shelter
as I take it in—my boys, the caged crabs, the heron,
the sky; a scent of iodine, salting my tongue.

Once slaves hid in these islands, scions of
of a tongue they kept alive for their own,
foraging boars, fish, crabs, and deer,
a teeming Eden just beyond original sin.

Nights over the ocean, did the stars chart
myths they carried from their far forest home?
Did they cipher barking hounds hunting within
the tidal winds? Or chant rhythms and songs

to ward them back? Did they holler praise
to the crabs and boars and fish for their bellies?
Pray to their gods to hold their bodies hidden?
And are they still listening, those Gullah ghosts?

Now, ripping thru the inlet, a giant wave
roars up higher and higher and thrashes on—
Two dolphins, fins, flanks churning the current.
We stare at their passing, seething to the sea.

The sky bleeds out its bruise; salt marshes swell
and darken the tide. Trudging off with their catch,
my sons are quieter now; as the night falls
about us quick and black, I tell them again

a history we can't take back.

Summers with the JACL

The picnic consisted of teriyaki, *tsukemono,*
and since some things were lost in translation,
rice balls. Three-legged races before the rain broke
and a raffle where I won a gallon of shoyu.

"*Nihonjin* or *hakujin?*" was a question I'd hear
but never knew exactly what it meant
though I hunted for the latter so many years
I wed one: a shiksa and a daughter of Rachel too.

George seemed a quicker moniker than Mas;
Mary outran Michiko. What kanji
you were born with didn't matter. Or years
in the desert, the mountains, the Arkansas swamp.

Years later I wrote my first poem about my *ojī-chan*
—whom I never called *ojī-chan*—in a room
where rain poured through the ceiling
in a metal bucket, not knowing that wasn't an end

but the beginning of so many lost worlds
as the leaking heavens still pour down
and shout to my mother and father
hopping to the finish line—*Go, go, go. . . .*

My Son at Ninth Grade

Overnight grown so towering, head wooly
with long curls, he'll stare me down eye
to eye. A black wisp over his lip he

won't shave. Hip-hop on iPod, beats
on Garage Band, poems on his Mac
book. And nights beneath the sheets

whispering through his cell to Yasmine,
a twenty-first-century down low romance
her father and brothers would shut down

like a house of plague . . . if they discovered.
I pass his door and his voice lowers.
What does she see in him and he in her?

Only it's not sight, there in the dark,
but the words shuttling between them,
old as Romeo and Juliet, Sharks

and Jets, Buddha and Muhammad
and the mad crazy years we live in
where this young love fights to flourish.

(Two weeks later her brother shouts
the alarm to her father and mother. Now
there's a line that cannot be crossed,

and still I hear my son behind his door
weeping and whispering in the dark,
voices on the line, their secrets abhorred.)

Once a white boy fell in love with my aunt.
Slipped to the camps, she never kissed him again.
Ojī-san disapproved. Still from Japan.

Five young Somali men shot or knifed
last year in our precinct. Others vanished
to Mogadishu, warlords, civil strife.

The FBI, the police, what do they know?
Fathers, mothers, where's your daughter, your son?
Children, all this began so long ago.

Tonight as I make our bed, my son sneaks
in, leaps my back with his heavy new body;
and with war yelps wrestles me to the sheets.

Of course I don't let him beat me. Grunting
back, I toss him off like the years, grapple
his torso down, pinion each young wing,

though even as he cries out *I give, I give,*
assenting to the father, I cannot grip
him tight enough, I cannot let go.

The Left Panel of the Diptych Speaks

With my black pointed hood
and my raggedy black gown, its tatters
like the Wicked Witch might sport
before she hops on her broom
to write the sky in black smoke,
Surrender Dorothy!—I could be
holding out my hands for a trick
or treat, like any American
child on Halloween eve,
if not for the wires that spring
from my palms to the wires
running up the tiled institutional wall
and the tall wooden box
where I perch as if on display
in some gallery in SoHo.
Just off to the side
you glimpse half the body
of a T-shirted guard or patron
inspecting his fingers—cutting
his nails?—as if bored
with the banality of modern art.
It's difficult to know what to make
of that, or how my photo
is paired with a pair of naked men,
one kneeling to one with his head
in a square plastic sack,
face to crotch, though the one
below seems more bent in prayer,
despite the hands upon his head,
than into mouthing fellatio.

Perhaps all this is a commentary
on the institutional nature of sex
or the costumes some shed each day
to enact their dreams at night
or simply more evidence
of how the plague of homosexuality
is corrupting our highest
organs of culture. At any rate
nothing in the photo reveals
what I am breathing in
in this hood. Or how my keepers
have dutifully informed me
if I fall from this precarious spot
on my soapbox, I will be
instantly and justly jolted
by fifty thousand volts.

Assimilation

it's '59
Apparichio at short for

my White Sox "Let's play two"
Ernie Banks at Wrigley

and I don't understand
these barriers these

two new kids someone's
got to chuck them so Randy

Hansen and I take on Jose
and Luis Rodriguez and I

bust Luis's glasses and later
he's crying to my favorite

teacher Miss Berman
but no one rats me

out cause I'm not
a Jap I'm American

American as they come

Peter Wu's Poem

It's snowing today, a few leaves on branches, the last guests who refuse to say, The party's over, time to go home. I'm thinking of a childhood friend hit by a car while riding his bike—the driver stopped, panicked, backed her car over him. First one thump, hard, abrupt; then a second, muffled, slower.

I spun out on the ice yesterday, twirling a five-forty, oncoming cars flashing closer in slow motion and blinding snow. No thoughts of loved ones. No life rerun.

The wheels gripped, I veered off the road.

I'm never going to die.

Peter Wu, smart Chinese kid, top of his class, good athlete, not geeky, friends with everyone. One of those kids so absolutely free of aggression or malice, a golden child. At the funeral his parents were devastated; though they kept decorum, I saw it in their faces, that utter anguish, all that was missing the rest of their days. In the program they printed a poem by Peter about a little ghost dancing in a haunted house on a cold and windy fall day. A day like today.

Driving in a car with three friends going over the blows of childhood: One, a Chicana, talked of running in a school yard and smacking her forehead right into the flagpole—nicely allegorical since her parents were undocumented. The other, of Taiwanese, grew up in a white Jersey suburb; one night neighbor punks gassed up a fire behind her garage and tried to burn her house down. The third talked about the Lebanese civil war, how at thirteen he held this outpost by himself, fretting he'd run out of ammo for his AK-47.

We all tossed up our arms, laughing, Okay, Tony, you win.

                                    ➻

Thinking Sun-tzu lately: This clique of rappers checking into *The 48 Laws of Power,* samplings of Machiavelli and my man Matsumoto reduced to four dozen precepts. Samurai and hip-hop. Blade to the beat box. Sun-tzu and the fresh Prince.

                                    ➻

Nearing solstice, dark so early now. Peter Wu, I can close my eyes and see him, playing ball with us in that field near my house, like he's still there, like the car never hit him, like his dad never had to rise at the funeral and read Peter's poem about the little ghost.

                                    ➻

Compared to Tony, I'm just a child. Never been in a fist fight or come close to killing even a goat or chicken. Some Rumsfeld or Cheney, some CIA ops, they've sussed those ancient manuals, doped the new ones too. It's a dog-eat-dog world; got to sic some pit bulls to keep us French poodles from getting ripped by those al-Qaeda Dobermans. A guy like Khalid Sheikh or al-Zarqawi, blading Pearl's head, slipping into Fallujah with utter glee, like a conventioneer off to Vegas? Hell, they'd devour me like slices of sushi, hack my nuts in a heartbeat, and I got the gall to say I don't want our hooh-ha grunts hunting 'em in Iraq or Tora Bora?

                                    ➻

(Neville Chamberlain be damned.) The following is not Peter's poem—

Top Dog, underdog, which would you rather be? Our lost boy. Who is the designated mourner. The soldiers get their homecoming, only a long way off. Pakistan, pussy, petro; the three little pigs. A roll of the dice. Melting ice. Red light, green light. That is no country. That is no civil war. Graceland. Dance, dance, dance. Our white toothy smile shining in the cosmos. We are not alone. Oh the enigma, the arrival, the fortress. 9-11/AK-47. Hut-hut. Digits deep in the soul's code.

Thursday, Dec. 6, a cold cold night. Blackness at my window. Temperature zipping below freezing. Arctic wind. Glad I have heat. Glad the oil's flowing. Glad I can write these lines of a boyhood friend, his farewell poem about a ghost.

Footnotes to the Book of Baghdad
(after Nizar Qabbani)

The ancient world vanished right before our eyes.
And the ancient books and all their dead.
Poems and prayers, curtains, sofas, beds—
The poet who wrote love poems now wields a lie.

A poet may stare at his flesh in the mirror
And find himself ashamed at sagging flesh.
But a poet who stares at his poems ashamed
Is never granted another wish.

Stirred by politicians calling out as prophets
As if they carried prayer in their very breath:
We went to war. We went to war and lost.
Shame worse than humiliation. Shame worse than death.

It's painful to listen to whispers of the defeated.
It's painful to listen to the barking of dogs.

We begged God for victory over our enemy
As our enemies once asked Him for our lives.
We did not beg the sultan for his wives.
We did not beg a halt to torture or to spies.

Sultan, you lost two wars. How many more?
But even if we took back our tongues
Nothing would return as before.
Bruises from his soldiers heal. But my son

Who sees the shoes that I have eaten;
Who knows my friends have disappeared;
Who wonders what I whispered in their ears?
He who looks in my eyes spies the defeated.

Oh let him never forgive or forget our sins.
Let a giant grow where a dwarf caved in.

A Surprise Visit

So father and son quarreled one afternoon
and on into evening. About gambling
debts and coke. About the Sansei's new
twenty-year-old black lover asleep upstairs
and when she came down, draped
in kimono and her flesh
as temptation, as she bent down
and her nipple spilled forth,
his Nisei father
saw only this witch, this demon,
and not a twenty-year-old girl living through
her dream time, her model time, her own years
in L.A.
        And what the son said then
I cannot hear, nor the words of the father,
but only their faces, in terror, in rage
beyond waving good-bye, hot
in their blood, leaving only this
medicinal taste in the father's mouth

as he drove to the mountains, and in his rearview
there burned out in the Pacific that
fireball sinking on to Nippon,
where his father once stood in a temple
beside his mother and the Shinto priest
intoned a ceremony which made all this
possible, down to this fatherly weeping,
dark drops on his shirt evaporating
so quick in the desert heat.

And the Nisei wanted to shout to the Southland,
to no one in particular: *Tell them*
my father once spoke a language
as difficult as orchids or roses or the ancient
songs of the Heike, with rhythms all its own.
And even as he drove from the sunset
he caught that pair
who begat him, standing behind barbed wires
as his steps in the Arkansas dirt
floated lighter and more invisible the farther
he hustled toward that bus out of camp,
his freedom leeching his presence
from their lives, dark and grainy
as his skin, as the short years they lost there,
at Heart Mountain and back in L.A.,
where their greenhouse once gleamed
steaming panes in the sun.

Tales of Hybridity
(after research by Juliana Pegues)

A man who roomed
in my grandfather's hotel once

seeded a child with a Native woman.
Up in Alaska, canning salmon

the women shifting to seasonal
labor. (The men saw no reason

to fish for strangers.) Iron
Chink the whites branded

the canning machinery
and who cares Nips

manned its welding
as the Native women scooped

innards and bones from
souls close to their own.

How does the living man speak
to the living woman who

flees the Christian missionaries
for potlatch and native belief?

Why didn't she choose her own?
Why did he leave? The heart

conceals nothing but
the heart, which is invisible

to history but never
the body. Issei. Tlingit.

Hiding in plain sight.
A baby called China Jim.

Recall May as a streak
into heat. A tryst

in the fields. Jesus
and a Jap girl. Sighs

in the gathering dusk
and the first weeds.

Tell me a story
in seventeen syllables.

Write a window
where his face appears

and she turns
like a whispered

promise: how skin
simmers as

summer enters
strawberries ripen

and mother's haiku
look away a moment

and father mutters
hayaku, hayaku over

fruit and sorrow
in equal proportions.

Or: half and half.
An impossible notion.

Once there was a house
in the suburbs.

My father recalled
no internment, though

there were loyalty
oaths he signed. Just

a blank sheet
as if he ran away

and never returned.
Me? I wished only

kisses from white girls
and the separation

that exists in a room
where two lovers

give in to their
ghostly embrace.

We were a colonized people.
We were a colonizing people.

We were never a people.
A nation. A tribe.

My father learns English
before I can be born.

I learn Japanese
to forget who I am.

And our faces turn
to history

strangers to the happa
children who

slam doors
in anger

or exuberant joy
running through my home

J.A. Songs for Richard Pryor

You grow up in a whorehouse.
Crack.
       Or within
internment.
            Shō

ga nai.
       It's just
different.

Tell the tale
of the drunk on the corner
directing traffic in his dreams
of a cop walking his beat or
James Brown twisting
a shout that gave birth
to funk and hip-hop and the beats
between.

You can't speak
about that, say the nationalists
and the honorable Elijah
Muhammad.

Ali
with a black face

as a ringer for my father
who fought no one
as a GI in Germany
and never refused
whatever Uncle Sam
desired, including
the camps, so don't look
back, don't look
back.

◆

The barbed
wire of Ramallah, the barbed
wire of Heart Mountain, the guard
towers here, the borders for Bantus
and Gaza.
        Topaz.
Rez in the dez. Compton,
and the Big Easy. These
are not the same.
            Exactly.

◆

Set yourself not your house on fire.

◆

Why is it Korean
girls want to lose
their slant eyes? Why
is *Dictee* a classic and not
my own? Why can't I sing
the blues? It's nothing
but the Mississippi

Mekong delta, nothing
but the tireless chants
of the poor, prayers
to Jesus or Buddha, Muhammad
and the madras slum
dogs or bitches, I can't see
any end to this, as sweet
as crack, this terror, this
hate inside me I can't let
go.

No-No. I wrote that.
Famous Suicides. I'll
never be one. Motherfucker.
Richard Pryor. Praise God.

That Early Angel

Having stumbled from the strip joint that now,
years later, houses St. Paul's finest,
followed by a girl of pale dark beauty
resembling the young Ali MacGraw in *Love Story,*
wearing a navy peacoat
and beneath an outfit of spandex and sequins,
I lay down in the swirling snow of the parking lot,
the flakes, wide as contact lenses,
melting
on my cheeks my mouth the spittle dribbling
and my arms still flailing in the indentation
of an angel hurtled light-years
down by the lord. And there, in the emptiness
before Walgreens and Target, abandoned
grocery carts raking in the record blizzard,
I could not tell whether that burning lay
inside or without
or whether the A bus or the train to the far
reaches of the universe
had just whizzed past and left only
my voice screaming
You did this, you did this, you did this to me.
I recall the huge tire of Tires Plus, golden arches
of McDonald's, and the pitiful plastic streamers
of Bob's Used Cars as my head swiveled side
to side in seizure. Visions
of the dancer's humongous breasts
and the bong bowl where red coals
of hash hallucinated
to the cities of the plains, burning
as once Sodom or Gomorrah might have,

enflaming themselves
to the Lord and the long block behind me
where the patrons and johns straggled out,
one or two pausing to light his cigarette
before moving on.

And then like a thread yanked by the sky gods
or a new vocabulary lurching to my tongue,
I retched up jiggers of vodka and lime
and some molten excess
of a meal, skirting out
across the snow. Heaves up
my chest, my throat. Lips akimbo. Bawling.

Forgive me, dear angel. How it must have been, this hell.

A Mixed Marriage Blues

You threatened to leave me in that hotel room for two hours
Before you came back

What kind of threat is that

You said you'd move out but where would you go
It's twenty below

Two feet of snow

You said your heart is broken you love me all the same
I always blame you

It's just a game

You said it's better to end it now and keep our memories
You opened the door

I felt the breeze

You said no one would love me the way you do
It was four a.m.

And then we screwed

You said all we have in common is the sex
I wrote it all down

Our holy text

You said the end of the marriage amounts to zero
Divide it by infinity

I am your hero

You said I'm a shit and an asshole too
You'd end up paying alimony

Intolerably cruel

You beat your fists against my chest and arms
I held you back

I have my charms

You said it would kill you you can't take it anymore
I called you Jezebel

I call you whore

You shouted yourself hoarse and whispered your curses
You're just the doctor

I'm the nurses

You said one day it's going to blow up in my face
You're only a white girl

The master race

You said you're tired of my yellow boy blues
The same goes for me

So pay your dues

You said you'll never give up the ticket for the last ferry
You'll head back to the mainland

As if we never married

You said you hate it will all end up in a poem
Just another Ricky

Lucy I'm home

Things That Lose by Being Painted (a Fiction)

Pinks, cherry blossoms, yellow roses. Men or women who are
praised in romances as being beautiful.—Sei Shōnagon

I Overture: The Cocktail Bar

Martini—yours dirty,
mine clean. As if . . .
Lemon/lime, light squeeze,
a Jill Scott riff.

Peppered wings, cumin,
cardamom, salt—
Nisei to Sansei:
It's not our fault.

So exotically doubled.
Never X-rated.
Perhaps just a tic.
Ill-fated.

Dear, your face
isn't what I see
when I wake
each morning.

II The Sansei Other

Whether we slept together

or not. Failing to protect the innocent. Intrusions

of children, voices clamoring for food, iPods, cells, clothes

scattered on floors, milk carton on the counter. Good-

night prayers. Fevers. Nightmares. Dishes. (Holding off

the JA—impossible trope.) Comes an eclipse. These autumn nights:

A last wasp whirls at the screen, yellowing leaves: And still I write sentences

off the declarative mode. E-mails. Haiku. Download: Black

hair, insoluble eyes, narrow nose, shadowed cheekbones (forgetting all that white

Hollywood imago?): Looks

like a Nisei car, I joked at her clean floorboards.

She hit me. Just before

we first kissed.

An open book
is also night—

In S.F., where our ojī-chan
slept in Angel Island cells by the bay's

black ripples, a century ago,
we're lying side by side,

talking in my hotel room all night,
the conference and meals of Chinese and Thai finished,

panels on misogyny, queer narratives, camp memories,
woman warrior and chickencoop chinaman, yin

and yang. You tossed
your coat over the chair; something

manly or
incorrigible

in that
gesture.

An old story. Married. Not to each other.

Except: These bodies. All I've never written.

Life begets life, evil evil, writing writing.

Reverse: life begets death, evil good. Writing? Silence.

No, not silence, but the blank page, the blank screen.

No, not even that. The reversal of writing:

The rest of your life. All those remains.

III   Love Letter to *The Woman in the Dunes* (or, E-mail)

To his eyes, recently exposed to the burning sand . . .
The woman was not there . . . her matching aquamarine kimono
And mintlike freshness . . . wild fancies . . . "Tomorrow?"
He chuckled. "Tomorrow won't be a problem. . . ."

Dear ——

    I had a strange dream the other night where we were in a situation like MTV *Real World*. (Yes, obviously I'm watching too much television, but hey, watching *Real World* with your teenage daughter is one of the few ways I can bond with her.) I was also taking some codeine so that may have something to do with it. Unfortunately I didn't wake up and write a Kubla Khan.

    I did have the sense in the dream of us being close and yet not close. And I think I challenged you in some way on that.

    I woke and started analyzing *The Surreal Life* psycho/mythically, which is really an absurd thing to do with a show which contains Ron Jeremy, Vanilla Ice, Tammy Faye and Erik Estrada, along with a member of *Bay Watch* and someone from *Real World*. But the girl from *Real World* so needed to work out some father things and in a strange sort of way Ron, Vanilla, and Erik provided three faces of the father. . . .

    I'm glad you're making some vows to be more selfish, to put some time away for yourself.

Re the rumor about you: Isn't it strange that we're now in the Nobodaddy position? Coming in on younger people having sex (rather than having it ourselves).

I must say, in a somewhat out of the blue but related matter, that thinking of you has made me appreciate the Renaissance courtly tradition and its Platonic code . . . also Marvell's "To His Coy Mistress," if you'll pardon me the use of that title.

I was talking to A. about my taking up Zoloft. It does seem to have removed some of the dark edges of my moods. He says I seem to be less bitter, less focused on how I've been wronged or cheated out of things. Of course part of me worries that that outrage is the source of my writing, so what happens when that's not there?

Re your proposed anthology: The problem with limiting the writing to J.A.'s is there might not be enough. I also think that the way other Asian Americans look at Japan would be interesting. Chang-rae's last novel comes to mind. Jessica's daughter's fascination with *manga*. Li-Young at a dojo outside Kyoto.

. . . after that dream about you, I thought up a children's book about a young kid whose Japanese mother dies when he's young and he's raised by a white American father. He comes to a point where he needs to find a way back to his mother and starts to do this through various Japanese movies or perhaps anime. (Think of Grace Park as Cylon Number Eight coming upon her thirty-six doubles; doppelgänger for Korean adoptees.)

Sometimes watching Japanese TV late at night after a joint, I think of how the one place in the world where my body would blend in is a place whose culture is foreign to me. There's a certain science fiction feel to that . . . that's part of Murakami's appeal. He denaturalizes Japanese society, even though he's Japanese.

Well, I'm rambling. . . . Is there any way you can come to ——?

I'm home days now, so give me a call if you want.
Besos.—D.

IV   Haiku for an E-mail Attachment (1)

Fall: slant drops in wind
Jarrett's odd dissonance
moans for melody

face like my sister
and not my daughter: as if
that makes it better

ambiguous as
Jenny Shimizu strutting
slim as a farm boy

why do I want you
that's not an opening line
cold branches dripping

tell me where you've been—
shoes removed in the *genkan*
in the house we shared

there was no such house
you say no such memory
saa! why write it down

only these words to
recall your face in the mirror
utsukushii na

V   Unsent E-mail (5)

There's the book I was meant to write
and won't. Like my first solitudes, scouting
the fields at our suburbs' edge. Tramping onto

a small clearing, a fire's remnants. Washed
out photos in black and white, men and boys
naked, wrestling with each other. Sucking

each other. All that's easier. Not mine. And yet
this hot tropical light came crashing down,
so thick I could guzzle it. Like the belief

I'd never have a lover. That each woman
in this alien story, not knowing these characters
or where she was, well, what could she

possibly prize in my face lying beside her?
And so
I sat in my room, alone, in a house that wasn't.

At night walked through rooms enduring
car lights from the road, sliding the wall.
And a woman somewhere else sleeping.

I played piano. The radiator hissed. Highlighted
long tomes with dialectics and delusions,
exiles and bibliophiles, serial killers,

samurai films. All the while someone was
screaming, nights like Duras's *Vice Consul*
in the Shalimar Gardens. Who shot up dogs,

beggars, lepers. White colonials. Weeping
over the stunning Anne Marie Strether.
Sometimes I wish

I wasn't Oriental. Or, less quaintly, Asiatic.
My plain Midwestern origins, provincial Char Bovary.
Recent years I've written little. Friends

dwindled, as if I've moved elsewhere. I've
left the howling of dogs, Christ on the cross,
shoppers in downtown Hiroshima. A rice ball

carbonized to black seeds. Ash. Zyklon. Zones.
An open book is also night. Why fight it?
As if clothes of mourning were simply for widows.

As if the Old Testaments got it right.
Duras: *Destroy, she said.*

                    The silence begins—
I can never have you. That is what I want.

VI   Jalousies

My wife's been unfaithful. This much I have long suspected. But that she should take up with a man like that. . . . —Milán Füst, The Story of My Wife

A woman clicks through the bar parking lot, hand
in hand with another man, in

and out of shadows and streetlights. At the far end, in the shadows,
her husband watches. They know—or do not know—

he is watching. The two kiss. In that moment
it's the husband who ages more than the lovers, knowing

the other does not matter
in the particular—who he is, his name, his accent—

only that she knows he is watching . . . despite
a car door slamming, startling them all.

A white man married to a Japanese American woman.

(Or vice versa.)

Duras again:

"*Destroy* is made up structurally of people watching each other at different
levels. . . . Someone is watching . . . and is watched by someone else, who
in turn is observed by a third party, and the narrator . . . sees what these
watching eyes see."

Her husband read the e-mails. Threatened to call my wife.

"She already knows," she shouted back. Him looming there enraged

phone in his fist. He

moved out shortly afterwards. Couples

continued. Or

did not. An old story.

VII   Alternative *Précis*

Well then. Take the story of a couple on a night on the town who wander into the local gay bar and drink too much, way more than usual, and they are serious drinkers. They emerge with another couple they've just met and the four of them end up in a hotel room, each holding a drink from the hotel bar. In five minutes they are all naked. In ten minutes one wife is in the bathroom throwing up. The other is on the bed and between her writhing, thinks, two dicks, isn't this how it's supposed to be? As for her husband, well, he's not even thinking at all.

After the other couple finally stumbles out, the wife on the bed looks up at her husband and neither says a thing. They get up and leave. As if it never happened.

For a week more neither speaks of it.

Two years later, she's in a hotel room in another city with four black men. Her husband's at home. She calls him up amidst the festivities. And he likes the call.

You cannot imagine the thrill of being a white man's sexual nightmare.

resigned to your silence
delighted by your speaking
what do I write now

were I there with you
shutting the door behind me
would we be alone

(something moves faster
than either of us can know
—I wish it weren't so)

e-mail Japan or
you: it returns as kanji
indecipherable

IX Lust/Caution/Film (First *Précis*)

If she sleeps with the agent of the puppet Wang Ching-wei

In the blue cheongsam bought by Mr. Yee

Leaving the table of mahjong wives, the tiles clicking

As he rips the dress, turns her over

"You should get me an apartment. . . . "

All this an act (Shanghai, 1942)

We've been spies so many years

"Run" she whispers and he knows:

Assassins are waiting out in the street

Porno of the *Pure* (starring Asa Akira & Keni Styles)

In the Realm of the Senses (dir. Nagisa Ōshima): Versions

of Sada Abe and the lover she strangled and dismembered—

Soldiers bound for Manchuria tramp a bridge in the rain

The lovers beneath their umbrella watching them pass

A dog howling in the daytime. A wickerwork fishnet in spring. A red plum-blossom dress in the Third or Fourth Months. A lying-in room when the baby has died. A cold, empty brazier. An ox-driver who hates his oxen. A scholar whose wife has one girl child after the other.

—Back to *The Pillow Book*. These Depressing Things.

X   Diptych

Under certain conditions, if there is
no wind, if the lake's surface

remains absolutely still, the temperature there
may move beneath

zero degrees Celsius and still
not freeze. As if the water forgets

its proper response. Even a few degrees
more may occur, entering

a new unknown state: "And that's
how I first felt

watching her
with another."

What I've noticed

is that white men with Asian women recoil, at times

violently, to my presence. Interesting to see them

inhabit an inferiority

they can't control. As

for the first time . . .

XI Love/Caution/History (or, Fictional Versions 3, 11, 16)

I *can* see us in another generation. In moments, years. A foreign

film: Time, pronounced Hawking, vanishes

in a hole and never comes back. And yet:

Marriage is marriage. There's no justice to it.

over and over make love drench their bodies in sweat sexual
emissions rest eat make love again again do not let the
chambermaid clean the futon coiled in this small room
shut off (in the realm of the senses/empire of signs/so pure)
by shoji she mounts him scarf winds his neck twists to
this oblivion moan tells him she feels him jump in-
side her looks down doesn't respond calls to him doesn't
respond slides off cups him carves him in her palm brushes
her name in blood upon his chest soon wandering out
in the streets in the rain at night bearing like a farm woman
procession in ancient fertility rites passes soldiers crossing
a bridge as the city sleeps Manchuria falls wars in Asia
rage 1936 1974 2009 when did you first see it when did
ai Kichizo Ishida *no* Sada Abe *ai no corrida*

ha—*shakuhachi*
is it orientalism
what i feel here

sampling basho
not very original
these haiku for you

we don't get two lives
there's never one solution
red leaf veins sunlight

Mishima's *Forbidden Colors*. Streets of postwar Tokyo. Gay bars. Trysts in parks.

Black marketeers, G.I.'s. Fallen aristocrats. And yet it's always

Edo, isn't it?—

"Yuichi sat in the bay window wearing the new suit given him by Mrs. Kaburagi, and the early winter sun coming through the windows like streaming water made the black-lacquered waves of his hair glisten. He saw no seasonal flowers in the room—not a sign of life anywhere. There was only a black marble mantel clock gloomily keeping time. Yuichi reached for the old leather-bound foreign book on the table at hand. It was a volume of Pater's Miscellaneous Studies, *published by Macmillan. Here and there in* Apollo in Picardy *were Shunsuke's underlinings. Beside it were the two volumes of Ōjōyōshū—the* Texts on Death—*and an oversize edition of Aubrey Beardsley prints."*

—O Japan. O Lust/Caution. O Science Fiction. O Mrs. Kaburagi.

Kabuki-chō again. When I called Mayumi she wasn't there. I thought I might reach her at work. But trying to find the hostess bar where I first met her, I seem to have lost my way.

I've turned a corner which looks familiar and should put me in the right direction, but instead of the glaring sex trade of peep shows and sex barkers and neon blaring various off-color suggestions, I'm confronted with a somewhat eerie empty street—tiny bars and mahjong parlors and tea rooms, entrances with ivy vines and tinny loudspeakers piping samisen and koto music, traditional tunes that seem so out of place amidst the neon po-mo sex trade of the area. Descending through the winter dusk I can still catch the stench of trash and alcohol, ramen stands from the other streets, but the street itself looks dead, like a ghost town out of some fifties Japanese movie, the Nihon version of the Twilight Zone.

Suddenly, a gravelly voice calls out loudly behind me, almost as if it's in distress. I wheel. An old *obā-san,* beckoning me from the entrance of her tea parlor. *Kite kudasai, kite kudasai.* Most likely she's got a *kirei musume* to show me, and that's not what I'm here for. *Gomen nasai,* I tell her; motion that I have to keep going.

We're seated on the floor in a small room, dimly lit, surrounded by shoji. On the walls are Noh masks, all women, a couple with neutral faces but most are darker, more somber, the faces of a wraith. She makes a gesture towards the masks and asks if I'm familiar with Noh. Not very, I say. She says that in the old days people thought the masks represented real women. Now days they're simply masks. Theatrical props.

"But it's more complicated than that, isn't it? Women are always putting on faces, don't you think? And what is the English word for it? Makku-uppu."

The old lady pours the steaming water into my teacup. "You must wait now for the leaves to settle."

She's been working in Kabuki-chō for many years. "I came here from Yamagata, just a country girl, so frightened of the big city." It was the only place she could find work. She left behind her whole family and never went back.

Just like Mayumi, I think, only a half century before.

I ask her if the area has changed over the years.

Oh yes, she says, it's nearly unrecognizable from the old days. Only a few streets like this. "But in a way, it's never really changed. Men are still men."

She points to my cup.

I take a sip. Like no tea I've ever tasted, deep and herbal, smoky with just a hint of bitterness. I take my time, savoring each sip.

At last there's only the dregs. Leaves at the bottom. A fortune to decipher.

She places the cup before her, gazes into it. Edges her face closer, steeping in the aroma. Leans back and closes her eyes. She stays so long in that position I wonder if she's fallen asleep.

At last she looks up. I can sense the Noh masks on the walls, the darker, fiercer host of wraiths that surround us. Foretelling the future, I surmise, just might not be the easiest of gigs. All this *Sturm und Drang,* all this hocus-pocus make-believe for a few thousand yen.

What the hell. The old girl's got to make a living somehow; the body lives on long after its beauty leaves.

Mayumi, I decide, would be great at this.

"Sumimasen," she says. *Forgive me.*

And I know what's coming next.*

*Years later, having abandoned this novel, I realized: You weren't Mayumi; you were the seer.

XIII   Aubade (1)

we shall speak of it as dead

you might have written me

but in that more chatty American way

we share, unallied with

the pillow book or its lists

of splendid and unsuitable things

XIV   Montalvo's Dream

For you it wasn't Tokyo, Shanghai, or even San Francisco, but
dreams of Montalvo's cuttlefish. Lemons, privet, acanthus.
A café at Rapallo. A profile at dusk against the Mediterranean,
I'm filming this beautiful woman, pearls draped
on her exquisite neck, the nape
where lust started for our ancestors. Schoolgirls scuttling
through a piazza, doves scattering. Marble
statues. So much pure stone for the houses in Tuscany.
Sunflowers, like the color of your dress,
in our imaginary travels, crazed
with that southern light, mozzarella offered on the blade
of a knife, olive oil glistening
off white soft flesh. Cicadas buzzing in Aleppo pines
as we crest the hill to
a coast sprawling beneath us, rocks and foam
churning tumescence: Each of us burns a moment
to stone. Breathing nonetheless . . . So
the sea repeats its restless fury
and there's no one here to witness it since
it never existed, even
on this page. . . .
                       As for you you're
drunk tonight. I can tell that. Solitary. Not writing.

XV   Aubade (2)

it's just xanax it's

just a martini it's

just another day

you say to yourself

killing is wrong

Regie Cabico Shouts Across the Bar at the APIA Spoken Word Summit

"David you're so beautiful I'd love to sleep
with you but I'm having my period"

—a week later it hits: this his way
of turning me down gently

My Computer Asks a Question

Do you want to revert
to the saved document Love?
—Despite the noun trapped in my mouth
or the lies her lips tasted,
the anise on her tongue
and the stench of another
breathing from her chest,
with conga mad incantations
and the hip-hop glide
and all the dances
she's played me
like that chump
who can't leave the tables
though the dice in his fist
frost his digits; in the raggedy
run rhythms gone awry,
misspellings, mispronunciations
(Miss Congeniality she ain't),
in the kisses held back
and those given in jest,
in the K-Y on the bed
and the horizontal moan
she proffered another,
in the haiku I send her
and the silence she sends back,
hell no, *nan da yo,*
call it off, snap it shut, trash
it, just let it be, let *me* be,
I'm so fragged and frazzled
and generally fucked up

why would I want to write
there again. Yeah, fool.
I do. I do.

The Rape of Nanking (a Fiction)

There's a ladybug on the window
I keep raising, lowering
to sweep it away. The hills
of the South Bay, eucalyptus
and pine. Deer and bobcats, million
dollar mansions, and all
I can recall are my interviews,
prisoners jailed by the Japanese,
whippings, cigarette
butts to genitals, slices
of skin peeled off as if
unveiling an orange (and this
just those who survived).
I hoist these memories
to corpses stacked like a club
sandwich of death, days, weeks of it,
in the streets of Nanking. The earth
a raw maw for the spineless
Chinese who cried out, begging
in ways no soldier
of Nippon could conceive,
though they could conceive
how to rape any female
they came across, how to mate
two neighbors or a sister and brother
in public, before the village,
in their march towards massacre
and the meat of China.
                          I turn
off 17, past the Cat restaurant,

up a private road, the ladybug
still at the window
till at last my fingers seize it,
cracking the shell, liquid oozing out
like some strange sampler candy
and I foist the stain to my nostrils,
the waft electric, a wire over-
heated and smoking.
                              I'm there,
now, no traffic, thickets up
a hillside, a hum in my brain
draws up the old G.I. who,
spying my face at the door
for an interview, curses out "Jap"
as I back away and flee . . .
                              Fumbling
I pull it from my purse. Ah,
now I understand it. That phrase—
deadweight. The dead weight
of all those pages I wrote or
the phone ringing in the dead
of night, the accent almost
traceable—"If you persist . . ."
I want this story, I want this story,
I told myself, knowing
no apology would ever suffice.
Silly girl, you're a Nip to some,
a Chink to others. History's over,
isn't that what Fukuyama declaimed?
I touch the barrel to my temple
and seer the sky of Nanking,
faceless soldiers standing above me,
shoving us into earth,
and I am there, tumbling
towards darkness. I smell them

on my hands, crush them with
my weight. Cry out once
like the wraith I am
and squeeze the trigger.

An Abstract Expressionist (for Marilyn Chin)

Mostly I'd spend hours in the studio,
Coltrane blaring the stereo, a love supreme, a love supreme,
sax riffing and cutting, J.C. sailing beyond
bebop, beyond cool, swirling in and out of smoke rings,
and in that dingy little studio down on Avenue B,
five floors above the winos and junkies and whores,
I painted his rhythms, stroke by stroke, color by color,
whooshing up canvases, five, ten, twenty feet,
like a fucking Mack truck, a wall of color, juicy sax
notes, raining golden ghetto gleanings off Allah. . . .

Man, what did I know? Just this Chinese kid,
doing the art thing, doing the Village scene, hanging
out in bars, smoking cigarettes till I couldn't take
one step up those five flights without hacking up phlegm . . .

Well, one night at this party, she shows up,
we start talking, *Einstein on the Beach* or some shit like that.
At first, it's a little strange. She's
Chinese. The first Asian I'd ever come on to.
Said she was a nurse, man. (What kind of nurse
goes to *Einstein on the Beach*? I was too drunk
to even think about that.) Later, we're on the futon
in my loft, smoking Jamaican, I'm tripping on
Jasper Johns, de Kooning, Pollock,
all those motherfucking geniuses,
and she starts telling me about her old man, how *his* old man
died when he was a kid. And then his mother married again.

Only she couldn't take Hoa's dad. Had to ditch him with relatives.
But a few days later, Hoa's dad took off after her,

across mountains, plains, rice paddies, all this Asian landscape,
and when he showed up at her doorstep
—how he found her god knows—she didn't say a word,
just clapped for some servants, and they brought him back.
Three times this happened. The fourth time,
she finally kept him. Who knows why.

Of course, that really fucked him up.
He grew up a gambler, cheated on her mother, kept
mistresses, even white women; Hoa remembered him
driving off once with this waitress ringer for Marilyn Monroe.
And Hoa's mother just kept taking him back.
She ran this Chinese restaurant in Portland.

And then, I lost track of her, it was easy to lose
track those days. Still is. Anyway, a year later,
I run into her at this Vietnamese restaurant,
and I suddenly realize, she's not Chinese Chinese,
she's Chinese Vietnamese. And watching her move
through the restaurant, I was still really attracted to her
—though I was the one who stopped calling—
and I wanted to tell her how my paintings had started to sell
(I was dressed in this Armani, knew I looked cool)
only I saw she didn't care jack shit about all that,
she was happy working this restaurant with her family—I mean,
it's clear how they're yelling at each other, it's all family—
and I don't know, I got this sneaking suspicion,
"That story about your father, it wasn't true, was it?
And you just let me believe you were from Hong Kong?"

She just smiled. . . .

Well, all this happened just before the bottom crashed
out the art market, and my stuff suddenly started creaking
like a set of mix-and-match dinosaurs. All this hip-hop,
downtown, multi-culti boho energy squatting in, screaming quotas

and conspiracies, the lack of diversity, all that p.c. shit.
You should have seen the crap at the Whitney. . . .
Man, I refuse to be ghettoized. Look at Trane, he
soared after art, after God, not some victim-shit message.
That monster black hole, the other side of the universe,
that's where I'm going, and I don't give a fuck
about the market. . . .

So, what would I say to her now, now she's making it
in experimental films? Man, they're good, aren't they, her films. . . .
Okay. Ask her what the hell was she doing with me.

What was that all about?

Wisconsin Hunting Season

Save a deer, kill a Mung (from a bumper sticker)

At the Stop-N-Go the clerk and customers
sport the faces of an opposing team.
I search my pocket for change,
imagine a mask that might protect me.

The bumper stickers brag of saving deer.
Leaves of familiar brilliance brush the bark.
If you walk there, an orange cap helps.
Cover your face too and keep it in the dark.

A fire in a clearing, a pot bubbling.
Someone climbs a tree to scour for game.
Someone shouts a curse; others chime in.
Now everyone will recall your name.

A tribe on the watch for foreign terror—
In the forests and mountains and plains
let this wandering be part of their lore.
Someone stole this land someone claims

*. . . The tiger woke me in the dark. Deep in the forest. Smoking. Tramping.
Autumn fields, no water buffaloes grazing. Once in my uniform. How my children
speak. How I do not sleep. Trucking car parts all night to dealers. Highways.
Diesel. SuperAmerica. I shot him; he sprang back, taking his claw from my foot.
Went back to sleep. Fleeing. The river where I swam, Thao on my back. Camps
in Thailand. The white man who said to me. Leaves rattling. Crunching beneath*

my weight. Chicken blood scrawled on a doorway. Yam and bok choy. What is this whiteness falling about me. So cold, so cold. The tiger. Smoking. A buck in the underbrush. Aiming at the target. My white sergeant. If I walk here I am not walking here. No, no, not that way. Distant voices. Where am I? Clouds overhead. Get back to the road. Voices. My daughters, home each night before midnight. My sons at birth opening their eyes to the world. Breathing. Wailing. The tiger behind me, before me. A clearing in the forest. Voices. Faces. White. Guns . . .

"Ladies and gentlemen of the jury . . ."

Kick Push
(a performance piece: after Lupe Fiasco)

Lupe, Lupe's my man. Kick, push, kick, push. That's me. But you know as much as I got mad love for Lupe, it ain't really like that. I mean, I wish it was, but it ain't. And it's not 'cause my girl rolls, 'cause she don't. Or that she don't like me doing my thang, 'cause she does. But it ain't always that easy, you know what I'm sayin'.

I was taking the train to the Mall of America. Going to buy me some tight shoes at Zumiez. I'm just minding my own business, my board on my lap. Up on the Cedar station this Somali girl steps on, and she's cute, but I don't pay much attention, 'cause she's got her head wrapped up in one of those scarves, it's like she's saying there's no playin', you know what I mean. And I respect that. I mean, there's plenty of others around, you know. Each to his own, each to his own.

But a little while these two black girls beside her, they start in on her. First, just sniggering and pointing at her, like there's something funny about her. Course it bothers me, but I try to pay it no mind.

But then, then they start callin' her a dirty Somali. Tell her she should go back to where she came from, they don't want no terrorists in this country. She should go back to *Africa,* back to where the monkeys are.

I look at the Somali girl and she don't look at me. Got her eyes straight ahead, like if she just kept looking straight, she wouldn't hear.

And I look around, 'cause there's adults on the train. Some white, some black, a couple of Native American kids way in the back. I keep waiting for one of the adults to say something. But they just keep looking where they looking, like it ain't happen'. Like they're the ones who don't hear nothing.

And the two black girls they're calling the Somali girl a monkey now, making monkey sounds and laughing their asses off, like they're having the time of their lives. And I'm thinking, shit. Shit. Man, I don't . . .

But then the tall black girl gets all up in her face, shouting, "Go back to your fuckin' country, bitch. We don't want you here." And I know, I just know, next thing she's going to hit the Somali girl.

Fuck it, here goes. "Hey, hey, leave her alone."

They both turn and look at me, like who the fuck do you think you are? And one of them says, "Fuck you, Chink boy, mind your own business."

"Yeah, Chink boy," the other says, "why don't you go back where you came from too."

And I'm thinking, Oh shit, did you think fool they was just gonna back off? What the fuck you gonna do now?

So I say, "Chink boy? Chink boy? What? That's supposed to hurt me? You're calling me a chink? A piece of a wall?"

I'm wondering if they know gook or slope, 'cause that's what's coming next.

"Fuck you man. Ching Chong Chinaman."

Oh Ching Chong. Forgot about that one.

"So you're saying I'm a gong. A musical instrument?"

I can tell they're both still really pissed, but they're also thinking I'm a little loony. Which I guess I am.

"Or you could call me a slope. But really we don't walk like this." And here I get up and start walking like I'm walking on the side of a hill.

They're both looking at me like I'm nuts. I take a glance at the Somali girl. She looks a little relieved. But also like I'm nuts too.

"Fuck you, you crazy retard."

"Actually," I say, "we Asians are supposed to be quite smart. I mean, ain't that the stereotype?"

The tall one stands up and glares at me, and I wonder if she's going to come at me. I'm not much taller than her, and the other one's kind of heavy and definitely outweighs me. I look out of the side to see if any of the adults are going to do anything, but they're all sitting there, just like before, like a bunch of monkeys, see nothing, do nothing.

And for some reason this really pisses me off. So I raise my board and step forward.

"But you know, the other stereotype, is that we know kung fu. And I guess you're going to have to decide right now whether that stereotype is true? But fuck it, it's your dice. Roll them."

"Sit your fuckin' ass down," says the heavyset one.

"All right," I say. And I plop myself down right next to the Somali girl. "You wanna insult us, go ahead, you ignorant motherfuckers."

But now the train's coming to the next station. "You wanna get off here?" I ask the Somali girl. And she nods. And we both get off.

And that, that is how I met my girl.

Sometimes I still wonder if I would've done the same thing if it had been two dudes. I like to think I would have, but I don't know.

Oh yeah, and it would've been nice if everything turned out fine for me and Yasmine, and for a while, for a while, it was. I'd go down to that park near the hospital, they got a little skate park there, pretty rinky-dink, but it gave me something to do while I waited for her. And we'd just hang out and talk and talk and talk and talk. I know, I know. It's not like we come from the same world. She's Muslim, I'm half Filipino, half Chinese, a real mongrel, and I don't even believe in God, though if there is a God I'm glad he made her, 'cause there's no one like her. I mean, she sees I'm cool, you know, especially on my board, and I did do my own little Jet Li thing for her that day, even if I don't know kung fu. But I got this sensitive side, like Lupe, I'm no gangster. And she sees that too. Some girls they be like 'Oh guys are such dogs,' but if you're nice, if you're too nice, they think you're weak, you don't got game. But Yasmine ain't like that. She gets me, you know.

Only then one of her brothers found out about us. Saw us in the park. And he lied about what we were doing together. Just plain lied. And now her dad's got her shut up, won't let her ever go out alone. Ev-er. Even to the park. All we can do is talk on the phone. And only when her dad or brothers ain't around.

And I mean, it's not like I've even touched her. I know what it means to be a Somali girl, I know that. And at first I thought that might make it all right with her old man. Can't you tell him we're cool, I'm cool, I told her. I wouldn't do nothing to disrespect him or you.

But she said it don't matter. I'm not Somali, I'm not Muslim, and that's that.

It ain't fair, I say to her, it ain't fair. I just wanna see you.

But. I can't, she says. And that's that.

I know, I know. I'm only 15, so how could I say I found the love of my life? But this is real, you know. What I feel. Sometimes I almost wish I didn't feel like this. I'm not ready for it. But I look inside and there it is. And I just know it's something special. How easy it is for us to talk to each other. How comfortable I feel with her. And how can that be wrong, know what I'm saying?

The world, the world is a fucked-up place, man. And I feel like my heart's breakin' every day. Every day. And sometimes I even think, those black girls on the train, they were right, you know. Oh not about the way they treated her that day. That's just plain ignorant. But maybe you're not supposed to cross those lines. Maybe you can't cross those lines.

So I just sit here in this park, listening to Lupe. Thinking she's going to come walking down the street like she used to. As if things really were like his song.

The Angel Muse

For more than a week, she slipped to my room,
clear-eyed as a moon in October,
not a cloud in sight.
                    Clear-toned as the battered
black upright in the church basement
where a young Sansei boy pounded out forbidden
blues.
            Clear as the knot in my father's necktie
and his face in the mirror, reflecting
on nothing but the day ahead: miles
of red taillights glowing on Edens, staff
reports, speeches for the senior VP,
a wrong piece of legislation brewing
in the House.
                Clear as the wing
beat of the monarch battering inside
my Hellmann's mayonnaise jar, seering
its way from that hidden valley in
Oxaca.
            Clear as the sheen of the foldout
and the glowing mound of a UCLA
coed's breast.
                Clear as the candlelight
where you stopped me in midair
above you and your beauty
and your whispered admission
you were still a virgin.
                    Clear as the rain
dripping down the headstone of Ojī-san's
lost Kōyasan grave, Obā-san's in Chicago, winds
from the lake beading that slate.

                                        Clear
as the eyes of the Indian woman once,
shining for me with red-veined sightings
of Thunderbird or my own
confusing face: *I want to show you my people,*
she said, so we danced through the bars
on Franklin before she disappeared as angels
are wont to do.
                        Clear as the panes of a nursery
misted with steam and the scent of orchids
and loam sold on the cheap to lighter American
hands.
                    Clear as Neptune and Venus and Mars,
the planets I named and placed in childhood
and lost with the numbers in Japanese
Aunt Miwa taught me from these blocks
carved in Nippon.
                        Clear as my breath going
out to the words on this page, so astonished
I sing them again and again,
                                    knowing
my dark face and slanted eyes,
                                    like no one
in my hometown, must sing this silence
of cages, amnesia, orchids, angels and mud.

The Great Nisei Novel, Circa 1949

My father stubs a Lucky Strike in the ashtray,
the El rattling behind him in the dark
with the bawling Ogata baby downstairs,
and he thinks of that line from Stephen Dedalus
dubbing a bridge a disappointed pier just
as the famous Nisei novel vanishes before
his eyes once again, right there on the page.
It's late; tomorrow he'll deliver dry cleaning
for Mr. Akiyama. Flirt a little with his daughter
Dorothy, knowing all the while she's not the one.
The one is out there somewhere in the night,
like the last leaf of the season to fall,
and he hums "Begin the Beguine," imagining
a dance beneath a spotlight or walking the Seine,
scenes from movies, novels by Mailer and Jones.
Just a while longer my father picks up his pen,
starts to write a movie theater, a man in the dark
gazing up at a screen among strangers, Polacks
and Micks, a stray black face, trying to lose himself
in the crowd. Then the man's at a bar, his last drink,
smoke hovering like fog, and a waitress smiles
a toothy smile letting him know it's there if he wants,
though he'll never see her again. Later he raises
his collar to the wind off the Lake, heads for the last El.
A pigeon swoops, something drops on his shoulders,
and he curses the pigeon, himself, the woman, the city.
Knows he'll find the last train gone. That leaving
the platform, he'll glance up, spy an Oriental man staring
from a window, images of Guadalcanal flashing past,
like the train he didn't catch. . . . What happens next

my father can't imagine and he puts the pen
down, scratching his pockets for one more Lucky.
Smokes to the nub and calls it quits. Tomorrow in Hyde Park,
at a dance with his kind, he'll gaze across the gym
at a nineteen-year-old Teruko, nudge his pal Mas
as he starts across the floor, *That's the girl I'm going to marry.*
—And this is how the great Nisei novel died before it began.

Song for an Asian American Radical: Yuri Kochiyama

I open the door
and there she stands hectoring me

about Malcolm X.
Says impatiently there's no time

for *sumie* or sake,
exigencies of meter, rhyme.

She's so tiny, I'm so
unknowing, the fractions enormous,

all those years of fires
in Philly, Detroit, Oakland, Harlem, Watts.

Behind her the night
stalks its stars beyond history

and I know if I shut
this door each time she vanishes farther

till nothing remains
but silence and sleep.

Reader you may think
in the end I'll let her in. Don't

count on it. That's
why she keeps knocking

night after night.

Love Poem for Suheir Hammad

the advent of the shroud or the dead boy in the street
and there's so much air between kisses you can't breathe or
fast for holy days or nights when love vanishes and breaks us

and i keep your vigil on my desk next to my doubts
and i keep searching for you on the screen but you're lost
amid gray faces in the streets of gaza of ramallah

and darwish the adam of two edens got tired and left us
and he wrote a stone in nineveh my corpse beneath the iraqi sun
but I recall you hooded and beautiful in white and your eyes

as we danced salsa dervished poems inside me and this scar
i keep there breaks like a line like a wall like a vein
kiss me on my broken sing shift gather re-form a nation

and there's a discourse on colonialism that ends
visa denied *no beit hanan tutu* a checkpoint's just words
and i'm still learning to write past the american

and lost land that shouts holy or war or power
and you miss your people and i have no people
and where we meet mirrors language as labyrinth

borders within syntax that cannot whisper dove dove dove
and shall we sing muezzin shall we sing karaoke
shall we look for each other in olive groves

and rice fields behind barbed wire or towers
how the invader never leaves he's got to be manly he's
here in my heart with high celebration and hate

and *habibi* i go down on my hands and knees gethsemane
kneel by babylon brooklyn phosphorous burn come
rite come cult comes terror come blossoms of the dome

we've made too many misspellings too many errors
forgive us lest we forgive allah yahweh buddha shiva god
all capitals i'll forgo to find you at sunset my cedar

and tho when you flesh your dark lover it won't be me
i want to tongue *mahshi* between prayers and your smile
breathe *za'atar* your skin exploded almonds in your hair

as if clouds of cordite never entertained a soul
i want healed what can't be healed to write a love poem
as if no boy or girl had ever ever been shot in the head

Poets in My Youth

I recall Leslie Fiedler deriding
The allegorical mode of Adrienne Rich.
Rich banishing all men and me from the reading.
When Ginsberg started chanting a man started screaming.

One poet recounted how Berryman cropped a pass
At his wife; wouldn't stop till the poet cold-cocked him.
After the Cabooze on a night with John Lee Hooker
I slept with a blonde who had slept with Berryman.

Gary Snyder over breakfast talked Zen,
His eggs with sour cream, slices of wheat toast.
Richard Hugo revisited his years of drinking,
Cutting conjunctions from his ghost town poems.

Merwin's Hawaiian siren in floor-length white fur—
More glamorous than any of us could take in,
In addition to his tutoring Graves's children,
And chosen for the Yale by W. H. Auden.

Bly lectured me grad school would make me weak.
I dropped out the next year with seven incompletes,
Just before nearly blind Borges read to four hundred
(In my review for the *Daily* I called him Chilean!?#%).

Siv Cedering Fox brought her *Cup of Cold Water.*
A Scandinavian beauty with rumors of orgies
(Or was that just my sophomoric pornography?).
She read in the same room as stately Meredith.

Who recalls now *The Wreck of the Thresher?*
The Teeth Mother Naked at Last? Or *1933*
And the short typewritten note from Levine
Thanking me for thanking him for his poems?

D. M. Thomas taught in residence all one semester,
His boardinghouse bed creaking with groupies.
Mark Strand picked up my ex-girlfriend.
(Perhaps the prime reason I became a poet.)

Alice Walker vanished the night before her reading,
Citing JCC white boys at her hotel setting off
Fire alarms, scrambling drunk through the halls.
Her just announced Pulitzer/NBA had her freaked.

Poets who sang the needle and "Willow Weep for Me."
Poets who asked for weed or a woman in garters.
Poets like Auden, who drunkenly brushed papers to his mike,
Asking in accent, "Are there burds in your rafters?"

I think of David Ignatow reading a book in my study
And avoiding the party of those he was to teach;
James Wright plastered and weeping before his class
Before some chair—Tate?—kicked him out on his ass.

Someone dismissed Donald Hall as a *New Yorker* poet
(I didn't even know what the *New Yorker* was).
When I asked Christopher Middleton about the arbitrary
In his images, he scowled, asked for the next question.

I was so young I believed in poetry's calling.
Art for art's sake or nothing at all. Yeats, Pound,
Eliot, all the high moderns. Dylan's Welsh sonorities.
I missed the Black Arts Movement and Don L. Lee

Before he became Haki Madhubuti, though
Lawson Inada chanted bass lines in a small room
Where I heard the only published Asian American poet
I could find in Wilson Library excepting myself.

I was young and far from home. Or rather home
Was never a place I found myself. I thought poems
Could house a lifetime in a way law could not.
I quoted Doc Williams and Keats to my father,

Defended my choice of vocation as only the young
And ignorant can shout (later in his basement
Found his rejection slips from *The Atlantic*
And *New Yorker,* in what must be a family tradition).

Poets of my youth. Poets in their youth. Many dead now.

Poem for Patricia Smith upon
My Nomination for the
Urban Griots Award

If the urban griot unravels his hip-hop
or lyrics her way up from the blues;
if she shouts gospel tongues going off
creation from the gardens of Babylon
down Egypt's dark Nile nights, hell,
it's all over but the dying's the refrain I sing.
And if DJ Kool Herc or even Biggie & Tupac
passed me by like comets in daylight;
if my feet can't shuffle Motown
or squeeze a duckwalk off the floor;
if my tongue numbs before some
simple preacher chant, *you hearin' me,*
you hearin' me, sisters and brothers,
girl, I can't slide that music
up my guitar, can't juice my mouth
to a boom box like Truth, can't
maze my way through alleys
where the size of your balls cuts to chalk
on the sidewalk and hopscotch
should be skipped by girls smacking
Mary mack-mack, oh no, I gotta jump
back, I'm just a boy from the suburbs
and yellow at that, my hallelujahs
in my past silent as the Buddha. . . .
And yet, and yet—if
Yuri could cradle Malcolm's
bleeding body, if some VC
could whisper to Baraka
the song Martin prophesied,

if you could dedicate "Let the Church
Say Amen" to me, P.S., I just
might be there, humming,
harping and howling, bones
rattling and rolling off my
All-American bandstand soul:
So yes. Pull out the crossing over,
sip cups of *genmaicha* and chronic,
shout jittery and jazzee as Zen,
as those long ago years
we shared spaces with those
on the rez for that word, Jap.
Give it up, give it up: *This
is the song of the urban griot.*

Dangerous Trains of Thought

. . . and Marcy still can't get her Chinese colleague
to agree to a forum for writers of color
living in the 21st century on indigenous land,
and I'm thinking of how they planted

Poston and Gila River on reservations
and the head of the WRA, Dillon Myer,
after the war, headed the BIA, proving
the US picked the right man for the job,

and I'm tracking Sherman's *Indian Killer,*
and at the point where the protagonist
decides he has to kill a white man,
the words spark this jolt within me

and I think how this Indian was raised by whites
and doesn't know who he is, as I did not know
all those years rooting for the cowboys
and Johnny Reb, John Wayne

at Iwo Jima, B'wana fending off
Mau Maus, drums in the distance saying
we eat well tonight, white meat for all,
and I wonder if it's the pale poet reading

at the lectern his insipid poems or
the Fox ditto-head or the latest teen flick
hero with sensitive blue eyes, or is it
the white man still breathing inside me

I must kill just to see who I might be. . . .

IV

V.C.

Our tunnel rat is the smallest man
in the platoon. . . . —Yusef Komunyakaa, "Tunnels"

They pick the one most like us
to enter our underworld.
We glide in moist darkness
like roots and worms
and our bodies rank
with the stench of our own wastes
buried in this hole
and the air chilly
as the jungle steams above
ground, where giant demons
from another land march
and rifle the underbrush,
order flying vipers
to flush their flaming streams
across tree lines and paddies
scorching the earth bare;
leaving only this acid
that tears at your skin
and sears your lungs
and blood, seeding
the cells in your organs
crazy with ant multiplying
hordes of intruders
years after the invaders
have left.
       Come out
only at night
sighted like bats

or the jaguar
lighting the blackness
with the glaze of his pupils
and ear cocked to each
leaf shifting, insect
fluttering, chirps
and crinkles in the canopy
of jungle that was once
our home. Slip
like spirits through
their midst, beneath trip
wires, past claymores,
changing colors and sides
so that we are cooking
their soup or polishing
their boots or hatching
a grenade in their latrine
so their shit can ignite
their path to hell.
                Years
pass, and each year
new ones come, more
ignorant and scared
than the last until
the Tet we smoke them
running amok, body after
body, corpse after corpse,
so they will fear
such creatures who care
nothing for life, ours
much less the villagers
whose limbs we sever
in their rumors of atrocities
that match only
the reality of the pouches
some keep at their belts,

slices of ears like dried
slivers of fruit.
                    Of course
those ears were listening
and knew always
where they were going
long before they reached
the tunnel where we hid
and so greeted them
as they expected
with all the gifts
of the underworld
where the dead eat
the living not for survival
but to taste the sunlight
they will never see.

Tenzing on Everest (a Fiction)

I glimpse the peak,
the long hardest yards ahead,
and Hillary's coughing, stammering,
his lungs struggling for oxygen,
and I glance up at his fear
like a child pleading in his eyes
for another bedtime story,
those tales the English lull
their offspring to sleep with.
And so I tell him, *Sir,*
we're nearly there, so few
steps to go, denying
swirling dervishes
blowing past us, plummeting
cold searing skin from our cheekbones,
mine dark and leathery, his
a milky translucence
revealing vein after vein
beneath the surface. *Sir Edmund,*
Sir Edmund, the day's almost done,
you'll sleep so soon, you'll see the sun. . . .
Something like that I sing to him
and let him lean against me
a moment, a young darker Sherpa
and an old white man, the kind
of pairing Mr. Tinsley,
his useless surveyor, prefers.
I know it's not impossible.
Nothing is impossible
if enlightenment is possible
even for thieves and murderers,

as the Buddha preaches
in the sutras I chant each morning
in answer to the winds of this monster
mountain I climb each night
in my dreams, as I do each day
with this illusion I may wake from
a life or two or twenty from now:
The dharma I am born to as he to his.
Surely one of my ancestors scaled
this mountain long ago, as I have
in secret some months ago, preparing
the great Knight for what he might find
here: blackness and ice, ice and suffering
which the Buddha proclaims
our earthly lot. So why seek it?
But as the great Sir barks
to his followers, *come on, men,*
it's not so far, repacking
my words to him, the question
vanishes like a yeti. (Man and beast:
The fabled tales. Ghostly and true.)
Before we start up again, I slip one
more canister and pick from his pack
and place them in mine, knowing
lightness
and a new sudden ease will push
him on, force him up where
all the world and his future
lie beneath, proclaiming
the conqueror of Everest as I hang
behind, weight on my back, opening
the door: Sir Edmund, enter first.

The Psychic Sherpa

Everyone knows the image of the Sherpa who hauls the tools and supplies for the leader of the expedition. How this leader will be white, the Sherpa dark. An Englishman, a Tibetan. The one known, the other anonymous. The one lightened of burden, the other bearing the burden of both.

Yes, we understand this job in its physical sense.

But does it mean to serve as a psychic Sherpa? To carry the unpleasant emotions and memories of another? For one person to be weighted down by darkness, depression, madness, so the other may be lighter, happier, and sane?

Do people of color carry in our psyches the memories and burdens of our mutual history so that whites can live in amnesia—without the burdens such memories entail? Do we take in realities whites do not have to see and thus take up? And how does all this affect the mental energies we must put out in order to function in our lives?

Separate. Unequal. The realities, the history, we carry.

General Roméo Dallaire, Commander of UNAMIR
(United Nations Assistance Mission for Rwanda)

I

"Rwanda? That's in Africa, isn't it?"
The words of a nitwit; an incompetent fool.
Now it's this trace deep in my nostrils.
Each scent a face. A flashback. A codicil.

Whatever my father taught me as a soldier,
Whatever his father taught him,
Neither taught me the art of memory—
How to forget or let it dim.

II

I watched a Hutu girl pick her way down the road,
Her faultless dark skin, yellow dress in the sun.
She passed a truck stuffed with the vanished.
Stumbled and plopped in a puddle of mud.

But when she looked down her mouth shattered
The air like glass, and the more she recoiled,
The more the passersby stopped to stare—
Her dress soaked in a dark red oil.

III

There was a rat the size of a terrier.
We knew the flesh he'd been seizing.

Today in the grocers I picked up a guava.
The bodies before me, the market of Kigali.

Nights I'm on the phone to someone I know.
They're pleading for help, pleading their life.
Over and over I tell them wait, we will come. . . .
Shouts. Shots. Silence. A dead line.

IV

I close my eyes and see a baby wiggling
Beside the bloated body of his mother.
I pick up the tingly and mushy being:
What twitches there is a feast of maggots.

And even when the maggots jawed their fill
And skeletons bleached to white in the sun,
The images seared my cortex—her bone legs
Bent apart. A broken bottle between them.

V

Near the end I brought some goats to the compound.
I fed and watered them; they roamed the grounds.
I wanted to believe I could at least save them.
Wild dogs from the streets would not take them down.

And when the dogs breached the fences, I jumped
And sprinted down the lawn and emptied my clip.
I missed those bastards. But they did run. Turned
Back to the faces of my men. They knew I'd lost it.

VI

Yes, the army told me to rest, stop my testimony.
I thought without my uniform my soul might return.
I am still waiting—I let men die, women and children.
My boys, my soldiers, those smart-ass Belgians.

(Kill the white man with the mustache,
Kill Dallaire, Hutus shouted on the radio.
Each white soldier marched as my double.
And still I ordered them out on patrol.)

VII

If only I'd hit a mine or an ambush,
If only I'd joined those I failed.
If only I'd attacked against my orders.
If only I'd run the risk of jail.

And if Colonel Théoneste Bagosora
And others are now shut up in quiet cells?
What comfort's that to the voices of Darfur?
Please shut the door. It's noisy, sirs, here in hell.

VIII

I am General Roméo Dallaire. Once upon a time I was a soldier.

Rock Angel: An American Version
(for Freddie Mercury)

Yes, I caught him on television once,
recognized his voice before I reckoned
it was him. He used to sing as a child,
little ditties about bottle caps, nails, or
butterflies, things he collected, naming
them the way another child might baptize
dolls or stuffed animals. And he'd
lose things, things you couldn't see
how someone could lose—a shoe,
his belt, his pillow, his coat in winter.
He broke his leg one summer flying
from the garage roof (I suppose
a lot of boys do that). When I asked
why, he said he spied a face in the clouds
asking him to come visit. A face?
Yes, he said, named Jeremy,
and he'd lost his shoe too.

Never thought he was odd. Just mine.
When he found that dead swan
by the pond, its chest speared by
some pointed thing, he brought it
home, weeping, like a child in his
arms, and suddenly he shrieked, it
shrieked and wailed, flapping
feathers and wings flying everywhere
and he dropped it at my door and fell
down laughing or crying I couldn't tell
since the swan swarmed all over me
and I was batting it back like a love-

heated mutt. And then just as sudden
as it rose, it passed again. Dead on me.
Heavy as a pig. I hollered for him to haul
it off but he'd vanished. Didn't
spot a hide or tail of him till dark.
(Still he shuffled back humming
as if he'd found another of his songs.)

A while after he got to disappearing.
First a day or two, then weeks. Just like
his daddy. Been five years now.
I thought of hiring someone but . . . After
that night on the TV, I figured
he'd find me when he needed. Now
I guess. When the phone rang,
I knew where he was, even before
he whispered, Ma, I'm in the hospital.
—Yes, hon. It's time. It's time.

Last Night on HBO

an absolutely stunning transvestite
boasted of always holding out a couple weeks
like some good old-time Catholic girl

then springing it on the dude who sputters
"No fucking way no fucking way"
as "Yes way" she squeals in delight

certain it's far too late
they've got that taste they
never knew was there

Crystal

1   Down by the Border
Trouble could be a black plume of smoke
bubbling over the city or simply
a cowboy, Semper Fi slapped to his bicep,
a smile like a hawk shadow crossing
his face. "Name's Shawn. You look as thirsty
as Vegas in July. Buy you a drink?" Toby
Keith on the juke, six o'clock crowd. Get
that buzz going so the buzzing in your brain
stops. Too many bills and pink slips. The ex
ricocheting with the kids for her mother's
or a brand-new badass to stalk their nightmares
like your daddy did (and his daddy before him).
Or mornings he and mom siphoned pseudo
from a boiling vat of cold pills, iodine and ammonia,
back in the toxic wastes of your childhood.
Only now that mom is me, the joker in the bar
sprawls on my sofa yelling at Judge Judy and sucking
a Mountain Dew the way I went after his member
hours ago, caught in a seizure of pleasure
that vanished like my prayers each morning
that all this will stop, a new day will come.
But each day comes just like the last,
and the cops chase all over the border
mule shipments from Mexico, aliens ticking us off,
while that All-American dream shatters
in our faces like a piñata spewing
kid after kid who never saw childhood
without crank fires searing through his house,
terror the drug of choice
only we don't call it terror, we call it

Home, home cooking. *We fought over there*
so we didn't have to fight them here—
isn't that what all them Washington folks say?
But the plague can pull in from any direction
and in the Bible it's whirling funnels of blood
or locusts, just as now it's AIDS or the powder
of God you snort up your nostrils
while the fragrant perfume of false paradise
flares in your soul, as if Satan's already
there waiting, so secret in your heart, pumping
with each beat, each breath,
and you can't take a step without ·
hocking him your life one more day?
Shawn yells to shut up the damned baby
that isn't his, and the one that is
curls inside, thumping my belly,
like the pounding at the door
one day when the sheriff finally reckons
what everyone on the block knows by now:
Welcome to hell, boy. Come on in.

2   Just a Tennessee Girl
I keep my hair long like this, thinking it helps.
Beauty, they say's in the eye of the beholder,
but I know what any beholder eyes in my face
and it ain't beauty. Nights, I still sift
those beautiful fires in my dreams.
The faces of my friends. A few shards of ice
in my palm. A spoon, a lighter.
Say how do you do to the devil
just before he lights into a liquid pool
of pleasure, soaring through your veins,
vanishing your hangover, your momma's
new boyfriend, that shitty trailer park
you grew up in till you found this hellhole
just far enough from Nashville so

you can holler those honky-tonk dreams
in your sleep and notch how tuneless
and deadbeat the real song goes.
Selma, Kim and I used to stew up
batches in their apartment, all
pins and needles as we poured
and boiled them chemicals
and I used to think, Shit,
I never even got to chemistry class
and here I am, like some mad scientist,
bubbling up brew that might blow us all
to kingdom come. Selma
dubbed us the three witches
and she'd twitch her nose like that blonde
in the old TV show, say this potion's
all we needed to set off on our broomsticks
whirling through town, gathering
whatever cowboys and horses we'd saddle
to ride all night long. "Double bubble,
toil and trouble," she used to mumble;
once I asked where that came from
and she just laughed, "You know, Josey, high school
and my daddy were both the same.
Never learned a lick from either
'cept how to drink and get high."
She was always the smart one, turned us
on to brewing our own (smurfing cold pills
one, two counties over). Some evenings
we'd drive down to the river,
resting a bit before our nightly battles,
the sun spilling scarlet over the mountains,
and we'd tell old war stories, laugh our asses off.
Then we'd go silent, like church,
cicadas sawing through the last light.
Selma'd raise her beer—"Girls,
it don't get any better than this"—

and we'd heave our bottles far as we could,
our rebel yells firing to the next valley.
I think maybe Kim knocked over
the pan, but it don't matter, the flames
didn't care, licking my face like the hottest
of lovers, my cheeks melting before his touch
dripping down my chin, droplets of
oily fat I once worried in the mirror.
Funny. Only singed my hair. Strands crackling
in between my screams I didn't hear,
only the hiss of Satan still whispering, *This?*
It's just a taste, child. There's more to come.

3   The Sheriff: Crank House Cleanup

You enter a house and it looks like any other—
a plastic hairbrush on the bureau, earrings,
perfume bottles, a cheap fairground bracelet.
Photos of people grinning as they're supposed to
when they're supposed to be happy. Or having
their picture taken. But your flesh
can't touch any of this. Just the plastic gloves.
And you're breathing through a mask and
everything's blurry as if you're swimming
far beneath the surface, the breezy salt air
an element you'll return to when your job's
done. But of course it's never done.
Don't know how we're gonna clean up this mess.
Kids, mothers, babies. Not just your hardcore Jacks.
Maybe I'm just too old for this. A while back
I knew every troublemaker in this county
and the next. Buzzards mostly. Just a few hawks
among those scavengers. Now every bird
you pass on the highway—crows, pigeons,
wrens and sparrows, blue jays, hummingbirds—
any one of them could have that death ray
in their eyes, floating within a cloud

of pestilence, concocted all on their own,
no help from the cartels or some pipeline
from Mexico. Home grown as moonshine.
But this stuff ain't like moonshine. No sir.
I still tell myself, Frank, these people are paying
your salary. But it's more than that.
I never said this to anyone but Gretchen—
I guess I thought of them as my flock,
though Lord knows I'm no kind of preacher.
No, it's like there are God's laws and man's,
and I'm supposed to keep track of the second.
Sometimes I think if they still respected me
this wouldn't happen here,
but that's just vainglory. It's happenin' all
over the country. Somewhere down near Tucson
there's some good old boy just like me
wondering what the hell happened to his people
and looking at these kids with teeth
worse than corpses a month in the ground
and the flesh gone from their bodies
like they just walked out some death camp,
not to mention so many third degrees
they're thinking of closing the burn ward
at Vanderbilt. Can't afford all those nonpaying grafts.
You'd think it'd scare the shit of others,
but they keep coming, moths to a flame,
and each moth's got their own sad story to tell
and some left little cocoons back in the woods
just waiting to grow up and find their own fires.
I slip in the kitchen where someone's flesh
dripped off their face like a dummy
from a wax museum and the black walls
won't speak a damned word to me.
What the hell am I doing here? As if
some nuclear reactor melted down, brewing
a wasteland one trailer, one farmhouse, at a time.

Christ, just go declare it off-limits for generations. . . .
Yeah, I'm a praying man.
But I stopped believing in Satan long ago.
He was like Santa Claus or the tooth fairy.
Now I wonder. Satan ain't the same thing, is he?

Isamu Noguchi: Fragments from an Unwritten Memoir

Conceptions (1902)

What was it like when they first met?

My father was fluent in English, already penning translations of the Symbolists. My mother, just graduated from Bryn Mawr, found few *prêt-à-porter* models around her. No Colette, no Virginia Woolf, no Edna St. Vincent Millay or Djuna Barnes. Woman's suffrage more than a decade away.

In New York that summer, he would have seen her as exotic, assured, part of a culture he wanted to absorb. They meet at a party of writers and artists. She sits on a windowsill, gazing down at the street, the last daylight. Her dress white, her cheeks slightly sunburned. He notices her dark chignoned hair, the sprinkled freckles, her long elegant nose. And her eyes, steel-gray with a blue glimmer.

She is a woman who grows easily bored, who hates the familiar, who has already rejected much of her past. She works as a reporter for a small newspaper. Her grandfather shipped to the States during an Irish famine. Her father owns a store in upstate New York. She's working on a novel, a young girl alone in the city.

She tells him all this. My father has already sensed as a foreigner he can ask questions, many questions, without seeming overly intrusive. The curiosity of a stranger in a strange land.

He does not laugh at her ambitions, her writing. He takes her seriously in a way American men do not. He tells her of *The Tale of Genji,* the man of many lovers, the world's first novel. One of our classics, he tells her. It was written by a woman.

He tells her too of *The Pillow Book of Sei Shōnagon.* The lists of the things the author finds coarse and unmannerly. Things elegant and singular. Frightful things. The intrigues of that court.

They talk about Shakespeare, *Hamlet, Richard the III, Othello.* How life in such courts must be similar all about the globe. The lies, the deceit, the use of innuendos. *Othello* intrigues him, her description of it. He has not read the play, its violent general with his towering jealousy, his innocent wife, who disobeys her father, who marries against her father's wishes.

By the evening's end, they both sense what's happening.

The rest I cannot imagine.

The bodies that begot me. How they came together, how they split apart.

Childhood in Nippon (1910)

At a certain point, I could no longer recall my father's face. He appeared only in stray, fleeing images, in flashes in a dream. My father scooping rice with his chopsticks from a raku bowl. The opening of a shoji, my father's face. The shoes of my father in the *genkan*. The voices of my mother and father behind the paper screen, arguing.

In Ōmori, after the move from my father. The back of our newly built house.

The boy holds up an apple and bites into it; the hard flecks crush against his teeth and the mother pats his head and says, good boy, eat. Juices spray his tongue. He looks up at his mother's face and it looms there, haloed by the sun. The corona a rainbow of colors, her hair a thick mane, her teeth smiling.

A dragonfly hovers above the pond where carp drift, dreaming of carp. The garden holds stone lanterns, a tiny bridge, bonsai, a path of slate blocks. Slats of the bamboo fence fall in shadows on the needled path.

His mother stands up and walks back into the house and closes the shoji. The apple she gave him is still in his hand, disappearing in his mouth. A taste of joy there he will never know again.

Later that night he hears her weeping in the dark. The sound drifts through the half-open shoji, enters the shadows of leaves on the floor left by the moon.

He knows and does not know why she is weeping. The weeping a story. It goes on and on.

The night grows large in the cedars and pines. A few hundred yards downwind the sea hisses, waves crashing against the rocks. The boy gets up from his futon and goes to his drawer, pulls out a scissors, starts cutting his nails by the light given off by the moon. With one cutting his flesh starts to bleed. He cries out.

His mother enters and does not ask an explanation, but bends down and takes his finger. She looks straight into his face and he thinks: This is the same face that watched me eat the apple, that put me to bed. Thinks: She is no longer weeping. Thinks: I am sleepy now, I want to lie down.

It is then both of them hear it. The sound of weeping. Each of them knows it is not coming from their mouths. As if the house itself. Or the trees.

Down the coast the ocean splashes on the rocks. The tide sweeps in.

Student Days (New York, 1920)

"You have no talent. Go study something else."

Gutzon Borglum told me this in what year? I was seventeen at the time, tutoring his son. I was to enter college in the fall. I worked in his studio in Connecticut, tried my hand at his leftover clay.

"There are those who have a feel for the material. An eye. You either have it or you don't. Stop wasting your time. And mine."

One of the great gray eminences of the period. Like a fool I listened to him, went to Columbia to study medicine.

Two years later I left for the Leonardo da Vinci Art School on Avenue A.

Cher Maître (Paris, 1927)

Late one night, talking in the studio. Brancuşi, the old Romanian, peering over his glass of wine. Brilliant dark eyes, white white hair.

—Do you remember that party last weekend? How they put on jazz records and danced around the room practicing what they thought of as primitive dance, shouting and clapping? They all have this fascination with the African, the Negro. You see it everywhere, in the music, in art, in the talk at the salons, in Cendrars and his crowd. What these Parisians see there is savage emotion and violence. They get to enjoy themselves as tourists without ever leaving home.

He paused.

—It happens with me too. They think of me as a peasant. Of course, I am a peasant. But not in the way they think.

I asked his view of the Africans.

—Have you seen their sculptures in the museums? Did they strike you as the work of primitives? Of savages? What I see is the gentleness of their makers, their sensitivity to their materials. The African carvers knew how to preserve the life of matter in their sculpture. They worked with the wood. They did not wound it. There are lessons there. If you have eyes. If you do not become one of these. [Making a vague gesture out to the streets of the Left Bank]

Oh but how I wanted to become one of these.

Things of Nippon in the '30s

1. A silk brocade.

2. *Bentō.*

3. Bonsai.

4. Beveled stones.

5. Rainwater in the rainy season.

6. Fungus like a ghostly paw on a pillow book's black cover.

7. The inside of her thighs tangled with his: strange tentacled creature whose hairy mouth scissors a raw and blood red sword.

8. Posters of Manchuria and soldiers marching.

9. The same soldiers who march past lovers huddling beneath a red umbrella.

10. Carp in a stream, pebbles.

11. A lantern.

12. Flags. (Boys' Day, the Rising Sun.)

13. His mustache dripping.

14. Her black sheath of hair.

15. A silk obi strangling his neck, her cobbled teeth crying out.

16. Chestnut trees out the door, heavy and wet with scent.

17. My father's face. His imperial fears.

18. The *shumisen* at Kurama.

19. A *yukidaruma* surrounded by children romping in the snow.

20. "Do not use my family name when you are here."

The Little Japanese Mistake (1935)

I once saw a photo in the paper of a lynching in the South. The image captured the aftermath, the living body reduced to a char of hard ash, dangling from a rope.

Something in me haunted to replicate that image, distilling its monstrous utterance.

When Duchamp's friend McBride reviewed my show at the Harriman Gallery, the first piece he mentioned was an abstraction of sewing machinery (a public works project for the Hosiery Workers Union). McBride thought the design a "wily" attempt by a "semi-oriental" to manipulate public sentiment for the union; the artist's tactic was "studying our weakness with a view of becoming irresistible to us."

The second work was a life-sized Monel metal sculpture of a lynched black man, the figure abstracted to a faceless head and a claw of twisted torso and limbs.

This, McBride dubbed, a "little Japanese mistake."

Friends

Cage: neither archipelago nor shark nor

even a single character

brushed on rice paper. The moment mushrooms

before the brush touches:

Bucky transcends the geodesic but
never the American.

Hopping bar to bar
together in the Village

like vagrants to boxcars
or a pair of grasshoppers

in a field of ants: mind like
a tsunami: a cool salt wind.

Martha on an empty prairie
eaten up by a rail line

as infinity
kicks up a heel over

her head: mistress of upside down
motion like a roofer or sparrow
hanging from the eaves
that never falls. Never falls.

⌒

Gorky the immigrant in a '38 Packard.

Paint vaporizes to a solid. Mother and son.

Such a hushed sound, a gyroscope whirring.

His endless chatter as we crossed the California border.

⌒

Frieda: Gold dust: Blue agave: Wound: Brow: Ha: Her lover

Poston Internment Camp (1942)

A desert landscape, on a reservation for Chemehuevi, Mohave, the
Hopi, and Navajo, each an ancient enemy. Out beyond barbed wire and rifle
towers.

I was the only voluntary internee. I worked in the carpentry shop,
hoped to design parks and recreation sites. Neither the camp authorities nor the
internees themselves were interested. Farmers and shopkeepers. Not my tribe.

I obtained a furlough. Walked out. Never came back.

The FBI investigated me for organizing the Nisei Writers and Artists
Mobilization for Democracy. I told them someone had to be for democracy.

I am still a deserter. Still at large.

Marriage (1951)

At the time of the Akari lamps, well on in my life, to marry the most famous Japanese movie star of the times?

Her name emblematic—Shirley Yamaguchi.

A classic Japanese beauty, our wedding a newsworthy event. Our faces plastered all over the Japanese dailies. 1951. The postwar boom just beginning.

Defying my dead father, the reformed fervent nationalist?

That's a bit too simple.

I did though embrace old Japan with a vengeance. More *Yamato damashii* than he ever thought possible.

Later even the American press took photos of the Japanese couple in their Japanese house—tatami floors and sliding shoji, the black iron kettle and raku cups. Sheen of our kimono, their brilliant patterns. Our wood-and-straw *zōri*.

I made her wear those ancient shoes at all times, even when her feet began to bleed. I regret that now, but beauty has its price. (She was a movie star, after all.)

We lived in a two-hundred-year-old farmhouse in a Kita-Kamakura rice valley. The joinery held without nails through traditional methods. I built a studio out back.

I was told the pieces I made there, aligned with the haniwa figurines, were too Japanese. Even for the Japanese. They betrayed, said the Japanese critics, a Westerner's fascination with *Nihon no mono* (things Japanese).

We divorced a few years later.

It was as if the marriage never existed. Left no trace.

Once, years after, on the late show, I found her face kissing the lieutenant from *Hawaii Five-O.*

Shumisen/Cenotaph/Stone (1989)

Fifteen centuries pass: this means nothing to the monument. Invincibly curious, nature entrances those stones: the *shumisen* marshals four mounts creating a tomb for the girl in the legend who found a pearl and slit her breast for a place to hide it.

As a young man in Kyoto, I first came upon this memorial. None like this anymore. We don't age so, nature doesn't age so.

Witness the incises in petroglyph on stone. Incises in bone. By these old graves one hears running waters; moss clings to the cracked curved flanks. The stone still ages its potent idea.

I recall a fire festival: the nape of night, huge iron baskets brimming with flaming pines. Overhead, a purple-black sky set a million polished stars. Like the pearls scattered on the beach once the little pearl diver unsheathed her breast. The hard thump of the drum. Her chest cavity booming her heart as she stole some secret from the gods.

Earth rears a rhythm in the solar plexus. Stone's an affection of old men. . . .

There's a tube now jammed down my throat. Something
narcotic slipping through my veins.

Forget that dream of some mysterious woman come to save me.
This nurse doesn't know a damn thing. In

and out of lucidity. Morphine dreams. Out the window
snow descends. December, darkness.

Sometimes I think she's beautiful, sometimes a nuisance.
God knows what she thinks of me.

Old stone face.
Old corpse to be.

Such casual relations
                    between earth

                                        and sky.

A zigzag path leads up

        to the temple at

Kurama.

     The course of a boat

          always

              near,

always distant.

      Paradiso, Merciful Buddha in Nirvana:

These ghosts grail only

       obstinate spirits: Grief

careens

      through a house

or, on a wind-driven night,

          driven out

on the roads. You'll not

      see me there

(though

     who would look for me?)

           Raku cup,

a rush mat,

    light through water

as it pours:

    this too

      can story

of stone.

They say:

He is a difficult man

to work

with. I am.

Very soon.

Entering

that stone.

Frightening Things

After wandering years
Basho returned
to gaze at his umbilical cord
pickled in a jar. Plopped
in brine years ago
like the frog in the pond
in his famous haiku.
Of course
fame meant nothing
to him. He stood
in the blazing rain
in his family graveyard
and as a crow squawked overhead
the stones proclaimed him
the last of his line. He
kept feeling inside his
straw raincoat for a missing
limb or the hole where
the wind and rain
flew in. I'll get drunk
tonight, he thought,
and his eyelashes glistened
as he trudged back
to his hermit's hut
to gaze again at the jar.

Zen Practice

deep in my poem on middle-age angst

but now my son prances in my study asking,
Where's Mom?—at six years old bouncing on
toes, and at my answer bursts out the room
like Big Daddy Don Garlits's funny car

long ago in those ads that vroomed
*SUNDAY! SUNDAY! At Beautiful Great Lakes
Drag Way!* and who remembers Don
now or the Crusher or Bozo the Clown,

not my eight-year-old bursting in
after his brother, asking also
Where's Mom? and I bark out
I don't know, she'll be home soon,

and he says I'm hungry, and I say Wait,
and he says I'm really really hungry,
and I say I'm writing, and he says,
and I say, and he says, and I say,

okay, okay, forget the poem on wisdom,
the waltz to my death, or even
the way my belly's starting to sag,
we've got to have lunch, and so I

get up and I fix it. I fix it now.

The Dream

I dreamed last night I was fucked in the ass. I did not see him, my beautiful
 anonymous other.
I sensed somehow it was a choice between us, he could have been laying there,
 his backside up,
only it was my turn, the thing to be known, endured. And I did not find it
 painful nor pleasant.

I felt no shame in the dream. Only a certain curiosity. And perhaps wonder.
 Next I dreamed
this former white friend, a poet of gardens and light, whom I left over race,
 and me talking
on the losses and failings of middle age. She opened her palm, saying, "Colors.
 More colors."

Now I could say it was merely the rectal earlier that day ending my first
 physical in a decade.
Or merely the poems I'm receiving and reading, deep into Sade, his
 mythological châteaus
and the innocent Justine, violated, strapped to a tree, men about her laughing,
 mocking her throes

of pain or exultation, horror or wonder, damnation or knowledge, she can't
 tell which, only that she,
in her prim uptight innocence, in her wanton stupidity of the cunning counts,
 the world's hot ways,
must endure visitations over and over till her training's complete, her comfort
 in the dark exposed.

This morning my son proclaimed: "I had a dream last night where the Lizard
 of Nature

grabs the girl with his tongue and licks her and licks her and licks her until
   she's poisonous
and takes her into the water. Then he rises up and holds her up to the sun
   until she's taken by the sun."

And so we dream.

Shakespearean Thoughts on a Stormy Night

The night unleashes dissonant music,
wind raucous with eucalyptus, pines
that batter to and fro like blades of grass,

as apples in the orchard thump the earth,
and deer hooves scamper through the underbrush—
a night ripe for the madness of King Lear,

or a father whose daughter, at sixteen,
is no longer a virgin, and who wants me
ignorant still, for all the reasons daughters heed.

Think how Prospero conjured and punished
the Caliban who accosted his daughter,
colonial babblings of a sex-crazed sire.

How Desdemona's dad shrieked and railed
at the hot news about Venice—a black ram
now tupping his white ewe. And yet, my daughter,

none of these plays capture me tonight.
For me, there's just the sighs of Pericles,
so far from his kingdom, deep in his fears,

who finds his long-lost daughter floating
the mists of years, unreal as a dream
or music that arouses the still air;

as still she moves more solidly now
into his arms and vanishing flesh.
The bleeding's done. O my dear, let me bow.

What My Daughter Tells Me

A spring rain at evening
and cherry blossoms plum-
met without tradition.

My eyes fail me. Wind
through the first buds, hard
as the nipples of young girls.

She hates my poetry
and my secrets and I
can't live without

the other. The metaphors
I've wasted fold my hands
not in prayer but

dismay. If the roots
drink in soil and the soil
listens, so many years

ago, my shadows rhymed
evening and sun,
cascaded words as a daughter

charts seasons, ghosts
in the body calling out, salting
her lips, her tongue my dusk

—But you can't say it like that.
You can't learn Japanese or coolness.
You can't know how it is

among her own. (She
sings like an exile
all you have banished.)

Beggar, broken king, mute
idiot, it doesn't matter.
Yes, you are her father.

You can't retrieve her.

Last A.A. Incantation

Yes, I'm going down to the cellar
where the roots thrive
and the shit-faced angels left long ago
and only the Buddha squats on his
pot smiling his sly stoned-out smile.

Just so a young Vietnamese friend
delivering on Cedar Ave.
told the mugger, *You going*
to shoot me for a pizza? A pizza?
Go right ahead, motherfucker.

The guy slunk off in the night
confused by death
in the guise of a gook faced
pizza boy, muttering his own
ending to the world.

Prayer

Forgive me God for my long silence & falling out of love with you.
Forgive me for posting no Christmas card & missing midnight mass.
Forgive me for allowing, as an altar boy, your candle to blow out.
Forgive me those hours I sat in the sacristy
between services, bored blind & teen horny, wondering
why I must wake so early to serve the holy body & blood
to three old crones, one bald geezer, & a middle-aged spinster.
Forgive me for not launching up to the breach when my draft number came
    up;
for not shouting, Hell with it, fuck the CO, I'm going to war.
Forgive me for doubting Jesus in the trenches, his finger primed on an M16.
Forgive me for not scrying enemies in El Salvador & Nicaragua.
Forgive me for not believing Right Reverend Graham
that while sex might be banned in heaven, golf will flourish.
Forgive me for playing golf on Sundays when I should have been praying.
Forgive me for lacking the humility of the lilies of the field
& aspiring to put a camel through the needle's eye.
Forgive me for believing in confession & adultery & psychotherapy.
Forgive me for the years of birth control & no condoms in the age of AIDS.
Forgive me my luck.
Forgive me for not stopping the war in Afghanistan & Baghdad.
Forgive me for protesting the invasion of Panama.
Forgive me for taking my daughter to the Spice Girls.
Forgive me for biting my tongue when she said they were greater than the
    Beatles.
Forgive me for never forgiving John Lennon for loving Yoko.
Forgive me for placing a portrait of my grandfather & not my father on the
    wall.
Forgive me for seldom calling my mother.
Forgive me for forgetting how she & I were confirmed on the same day.
Forgive me for reading over & over "Sunday Morning" by Stevens.

Forgive me for not buying enough life insurance or diversifying my portfolio.
Forgive me for seeking salvation in LSD, orgasms & weed.
Forgive me for killing Kennedy, King & Kennedy.
Forgive me for making them my holy Trinity.
Forgive me my Emily Dickinson & Frost & Edward Arlington Robinson.
Forgive me my worship of this minor art called poetry.
Forgive me & I will never repent.

God, do not forgive me, I will never relent.

Aubade

A wound is a blossom
but only to the living.
A May night, birdsong

before the first light pierces,
chirps out of blackness:
My daughter's angry at me

and her mother as I
was once angry at mine.
It's a way of crossing over.

I'm so tired now.
And my core's
all water, flowing

somewhere where the sea
can't find her. And neither
can I. How much longer

till I finally lose her? Where
is the first dawn wet blossom?
Who recalls how I touched

her mother once? Or many others?
How night is not always easy.
Nor are daughters. Nor are sons.

And how is it I've become a father
watching light sift slowly
into the daughterless dark.

Notes

"My Son at Ninth Grade": The Japanese term *oji-san* means "grandfather."

"The Left Panel of the Diptych Speaks": This poem refers to one of the Abu Ghraib photos that appeared next to another photo in a *New York Times* article.

"Summers with the JACL": JACL, Japanese American Citizens League; "*Nihonjin* or *hakujin*?" "Japanese or white?"

"Tales of Hybridity": Issei, first-generation Japanese American; *hayaku,* "hurry."

"J.A. Songs for Richard Pryor": *Shō ga nai,* "It can't be helped."

"A Surprise Visit": Sansei, third-generation Japanese American; Nisei, second-generation Japanese American. Almost all mainland first-generation and second-generation Japanese Americans were interned or imprisoned during World War II as the result of Executive Order 9066. Most Sansei were born after the war and did not experience the internment camps.

"Things That Lose by Being Painted": Wang Ching-wei was head of the Chinese puppet government under the Japanese occupation in World War II. In the film *Lust, Caution,* based on the story by Ellen Chang, a Chinese woman sleeps with the head of the secret service of the Wang government in order to lure him to his assassination; at the last moment she warns him that there are assassins waiting for him in the street. *Ai no corrida* (bullfight of love), Japanese title of the film *In the Realm of the Senses,* which depicts the love affair of Sada Abe (Eiko Matsuda) and Kichizo Ishida (Tatsuya Fuji), an affair that includes the use of strangling for sexual pleasure and ends with Ishida's death, after which Abe cuts off her lover's penis and carries it through the streets of Tokyo. In 2009, a pornographic version of this story, *Pure,* was produced, starring Asa Akira and Keni Styles. *Kirei musume,* "pretty daughter."

"Wisconsin Hunting Season": The Hmong fought for the CIA in Laos against the communist Pathet Lao; after the United States pulled out of Southeast Asia and the Pathet Lao took over in 1975, tens of thousands of Hmong were forced to flee to Thailand. The Twin Cities house the second largest Hmong population in the country. This poem references two murder convictions. Chai Soua Vang was convicted in 2005 of killing six white hunters and wounding two others in Wisconsin. ("Mr. Vang had told the police that the local hunters used ethnic slurs against him and fired at him before he started shooting. A police statement by a hunter wounded in the incident makes no mention of ethnic slurs," *New York Times,* November 27, 2004.)

Vang had been trained as a marksman in the California National Guard. A couple years later in Wisconsin, a white hunter, James Nichols, was convicted of killing a

Hmong hunter, Cha Vang ("A white hunter accused of killing a Hmong immigrant during a dispute in the woods was motivated in part by prejudice and did not act in self-defense as he claimed, a prosecutor told jurors Tuesday," *Los Angeles Times*, October 3, 2007).

"Song for an Asian American Radical: Yuri Kochiyama," "Poem for Patricia Smith Upon My Nomination for an Urban Griots Award": Yuri Kochiyama is a Japanese American human rights activist who moved to Harlem after being interned during World War II at the Jerome, Arkansas, camp (where my father was also interned). She was a friend of Malcolm X's and a member of his Organization of Afro-American Unity, formed after he left the Nation of Islam. Kochiyama was present at the Audubon Ballroom when Malcolm X was assassinated and held him in her arms as he was dying (her presence there was not part of Spike Lee's film on Malcolm). During the Paris Peace Talks negotiations between the United States and North Vietnam to end the war (which Americans call the War in Vietnam and the Vietnamese call the American War), a member of the North Vietnamese delegation told Amiri Baraka that the Vietnamese took inspiration from the struggle of African Americans during the civil rights movement.

"Dangerous Trains of Thought": Dillon S. Myer was the head of the War Relocation Authority, which oversaw the internment of approximately one hundred twenty thousand Japanese Americans during World War II. After the war he was appointed head of the Bureau of Indian Affairs.

"Tenzing on Everest": Tenzing Norgay was a Tibetan Sherpa who reached the summit of Mount Everest with Edmund Hillary in 1953. In a previous attempt on Everest, Norgay had helped save Hillary's life when Hillary fell into a crevasse. Norgay later disagreed with certain remarks Hillary made about their climb: "I do feel that in his story of our final climb he is not quite fair to me; that all the way through he indicates that when things went well it was his doing, and when things went badly it was mine. For this is simply not true" (Tenzing Norgay and James Ramsey Ullman, *Man of Everest: The Story of Tenzing Norgay, Sir Edmund Hillary's Sherpa*, 1955).

"General Roméo Dallaire, Commander of UNAMIR": In 1993, Roméo Dallaire was appointed the force commander of UNAMIR, the United Nations Assistance Mission for Rwanda. Dallaire's mission was to assist in the implementation of the Arusha Accords, which ended a three-year civil war between the government of Rwanda and the rebel Rwandan Patriotic Front. When the Hutu extremists in the Rwandan government and in the general population began to persecute and kill Tutsis, Dallaire's ability to protect the Tutsis was limited by the United Nations; he and his men were kept, for example, from seizing weapons shipped to Kigali, weapons which they knew were to be used for an attack on Tutsis. In 2004, Colonel Théoneste Bagosora was convicted of genocide and of murdering ten Belgian peacekeepers.